IF YOU WANT A
DO YOUR

A principal's guide to becoming a teacher, counselor or administrator

Kurt Karcich

Copyright © 2020 by Kurt Karcich
All Rights Reserved

Contents

Preface   1

Introduction   10

Chapter 1: How to Begin Your Job Search   17
- Networking
- Resume - Cover Letter - Completing the Application
- Deciding where to apply
- Create a portfolio
- Professionalism & Social Media

Chapter 2: You Landed an Interview... Now What?   40
- Do your homework!
- List your biggest accomplishments
- Review your portfolio
- Possible interview questions
- The night before

Chapter 3: Gameday   55
- Arrival at the interview
- Sell yourself
- Connecting with the interviewer
- What to do if stumped by a question
- Share your passion
- What questions should I ask

Chapter 4: Thank You Letter   72

Chapter 5: Second Interview   77

Chapter 6: Demonstration (Demo) Lesson   81
    Organization/Planning
    Connecting with students
    Command of the classroom
    Ability to adapt

Chapter 7: Negotiating Salary   92

Chapter 8: Handling rejection   95
    The Reality Check
    Never Burn a Bridge

Chapter 9: Conclusion   101

Preface

It was August 23, 2003. A few months prior, I had decided to make a career change. I was leaving the corporate world of sales/management to pursue a career in education. Based on my undergraduate degree, I was limited in what I could teach, but I was determined to land a job as a teacher and begin my new career! I was enrolled in the alternate route program but needed to secure a job in a school district before I was eligible to begin my teacher training program. I needed a school to take a chance on me as a teacher even though I had no experience in the classroom. I sent out dozens of resumes with minimal responses. After all, I had no experience as a teacher!

The new school-year was beginning in less than two weeks, and I was running out of time. On August 23, 2003, I noticed an ad in the paper (yes, people actually read the paper to find jobs in 2003!) for a middle school math position at Roy W. Brown Middle School in Bergenfield, NJ. The ad stated that applicants must be HIGHLY QUALIFIED in Math. I was NOT highly qualified but knew I could do the job. It was August 23rd, and I was desperate. However, I also knew the school district was desperate as well because school was starting soon and they still had a vacant position. I decided to give it a shot.

I called the school and spoke to the Principal's secretary. I confirmed that the position had not been filled. I also asked if the principal was available, and she told me he was on the phone. I said thank you, hung up and got in my car. This was my chance! Most people would have seen the ad and *never even inquired*. They would assume they were unqualified and move on to another posting. I decided to make a bold move since I was determined to find a job and besides, I had nothing to lose! And remember, I knew they must also be getting desperate to fill the position.

I arrived at the school and walked into the main office and asked to speak to the principal (I could see him sitting in his office). The secretary asked if I had an appointment and I replied, "No." I then directed my attention to the principal and said,

"Excuse me sir, sorry to show up unannounced, but I'm interested in teaching math and I think I would be a perfect candidate for your opening."

He invited me in and four hours later I was offered the job. Actually, I had landed a new *CAREER* in education! A little persistence, taking action, being prepared for my moment, connecting with the interviewer and BAM... I got the job! I will never forget that day and the joy I felt while walking out of the building.

Here is my recollection of my meeting with the principal:

I remember sitting in the principal's office, not knowing what to expect. I expressed my interest in a career change and my passion for helping kids succeed. Since I didn't have any teaching experience, I focused on my coaching experience. I talked about how I had developed a positive rapport with kids and motivated them to be successful. I remember the principal asking,

"That sounds great but can you teach math?"

I responded by sharing stories of tutoring friends in high school and college. Math always came easy to me so I shared that teaching others always felt very natural. I went on to say that I understood that not all students enjoyed math or found it easy like I did. To reach these students, it would be important to make math fun and relatable. There are many different approaches to solving most mathematical problems. For example, some students learn better with a visual representation of a concept. I also stressed the importance of engaging students in the content by making real world connections. While doing research on teaching math, I discovered that one of the most common reasons students became disinterested in math was that they did not see a connection to the real world. Even to this day, many students ask the question,

"Why do I need to learn this?" OR
"When will I ever use this?"

Fortunately for me, the principal was intrigued by me as a candidate and called in his math supervisor to join the conversation. The math supervisor was impressed by the math classes I had completed in college. I had a good feeling throughout the meeting as there was a natural flow of conversation. In a weird way I felt as though the two men sitting in front of me were not strangers. I was able to really *connect* with the interviewers as we appeared to have similar beliefs.

My good fortune continued as the math supervisor was a high school football official and remembered me as a former player. We actually spent about ten minutes talking about high school football before the discussion reverted back to teaching. After about an hour, I felt confident that our meeting would end with a job offer. I was confident that I could do the job in the classroom but in this case, it was really about connecting with the interviewers. After more than two hours of discussing everything from family to football to teaching, I was being sent to meet with the superintendent! After a long interview with him and other central office administrators, I walked out of his office with a contract to become a teacher in Bergenfield! I will never forget that moment. I hope everyone has the opportunity to experience such a genuine feeling of exuberance.

Roy W. Brown was a great place. I made some good friends and learned so much in my first year. The other 7th grade math teacher, Jim, was a great mentor, and I was like a sponge, soaking in as much information as I could. After my first year, I was hooked and knew I was destined to become an educational leader. I enrolled in a master's program in Educational Leadership at Fairleigh Dickinson University. I spent three years at Roy Brown before landing a quasi-administrative gig at Hackensack Middle School. During the ensuing year, I did a lot of grunt work, but was appreciative for the opportunity as I learned the nuts and bolts of being an administrator.

The following year, I was hired as an Assistant Principal at Hawthorne HS. I had applied late for this position and was lucky to have even received a call for an interview. I found out later that the principal had decided (the day before interviewing me) to move forward with another candidate and only called me in as a "courtesy" interview. An old friend of my family, who I had not spoken to in years, was the outgoing assistant principal in Hawthorne. He had asked the principal (who was conducting the interviews) if he would meet with me (as a favor). The principal agreed even though he was 99% sure that he had already found his new assistant principal. I researched the school and studied their website. I was also able to learn about the principal and what he valued as the leader of the school. I had heard great things about the school and the principal and believed this was an ideal destination for me. I had been a finalist for assistant principal in two other districts but was not the chosen candidate, and was starting to feel a bit frustrated.

I was interviewed by the principal and a veteran teacher. I arrived prepared and immediately connected with the interviewers. I thought the interview went well, but did not know just how well until after I was offered the position. After being hired, the principal told me the whole story. He said that he had already decided on another candidate but gave me a courtesy interview because of Jack (the departing assistant principal). After I walked out of the interview, he looked to the veteran teacher and asked, "Are you thinking what I'm thinking?" She replied, "I hope so." The principal then said, "I think we should hire Kurt." She replied, "I'm so glad you said that!"

I truly believe there was some divine intervention there. I was not more qualified or more deserving than the other candidate. I was lucky to even get an interview, a *courtesy* one at that. But for whatever reason I really bonded with the principal. I was prepared for my chance and made the most of it. Our vision and values were aligned, and I was the type of person he was looking for. In this book, I will talk a lot about the importance of preparation, and what to do leading up to the interview. Preparation definitely played a role here, but honestly, in this case, it was much more about **connecting with the interviewer** (which I will also speak about in detail).

I spent two of the most enjoyable and rewarding years of my career in Hawthorne. It was a great community and the principal and I worked very well together. I hoped to be there for a very long time. I remember one day toward the end of my second year, the principal asked me to meet with him after school. He had been a principal for ten years and was ready for a new challenge. I knew he was applying for superintendent openings in other districts, so I assumed he just wanted to update me on the status of his search. Selfishly, I didn't want him to leave because I really enjoyed working for him. At the same time, however, he had become a good friend, and I wanted him to be happy. I was surprised when he said to me,

"Have you thought about applying for any High School Principal jobs?" I replied, "No, I love it here. And if you leave to become a superintendent somewhere else, I would hope to have a good shot at becoming the next principal here."

He agreed that I would be a strong candidate to become the next principal at Hawthorne High School, but obviously nothing was guaranteed. He also shared that I shouldn't wait around for him because who knows if or when that will happen. He told me he thought I was ready to be a principal and run my own building. I appreciated the confidence he had in me, but I was not sure if I was ready. After all, I had only been a high school administrator for two years. I responded jokingly,

"I hope you're not trying to get rid of me."

He chuckled and told me that was definitely not the case. He also shared that it was his opinion that assistant principals fall into one of two categories… lifelong assistant principals and those that are being groomed to become a principal. He believed that 2-5 years was a reasonable timeframe to acquire the necessary skills and experience to become a principal. He was a great mentor and had prepared me well over the past two years, as we had discussed all major decisions together. I will be forever indebted to him for giving me a chance.

He suggested that I be selective and only apply to schools that were extremely appealing. He told me I was in a great position because I didn't *need* a new job, and he was right! I was very happy where I was and was in a great position to be extremely selective as to where I applied (this situation of not *needing* a new job will be discussed in more detail later). I did not expect to land a job as a principal, but I thought the interview experience would be valuable so I decided to take his advice.

I completed a search in my area and found a handful of job postings for *High School Principal*. After considering many factors, I concluded there were only two openings that were of interest to me. I only applied to these two schools. I received interviews in both districts. I did my homework and became very familiar with both schools. I researched their goals and made sure I was fully *prepared* before my respective interviews. Throughout this book, preparation is a major theme that will be discussed in great detail.

I was fortunate to be offered both positions! I thought long and hard about my decision before accepting one of the offers. **In six years, I went from hoping a school would take a chance on me as a teacher with no experience, to becoming a High School Principal!** To be clear, I am not saying this to brag. Actually, quite the contrary! I had less experience than other candidates, I was not more talented or better qualified, not smarter or more deserving. However, I made the most of what I could control! I was determined to succeed, I was prepared for my interviews AND was able to connect with the interviewers. You can do what I did! You can land your dream job, regardless of your prior experience. A strong commitment to succeed and the willingness to do the work will lead to your success. I encourage you to embrace the suggestions provided within this book.

Introduction

During my eleven years as a high school principal I have sat through hundreds of interviews. I have hired teachers, counselors and administrators. While the overall approach is very similar for all of these positions, the majority of this book will focus on teachers; however, the same principles apply to all positions and there will also be specific examples dedicated to both counselors and administrators.

Sadly, many interviews end before they even begin. I have witnessed hundreds of candidates arrive at an interview unprepared, empty-handed and dressed unprofessionally. These are deal breakers! You need to make sure you put your best foot forward as interviews are hard to get, and you want to make sure you make a great (first) impression on your big day. There is a ton of information online about interview questions and how to properly format a resume. I will not hyper focus on these details; however, I will touch upon the best approach to answering some commonly asked interview questions AND the most important things to consider when writing a resume.

I have yet to see a book that offers you everything you need to know from A to Z to land a job as an educator. I hope this book becomes that "go to" resource for you! I will take you on a journey that will begin with starting your job search and end with a polished demonstration lesson that will impress even the most critical observers in the room.

This book is intended to be *conversational* in nature, so please don't judge me as a literary expert. Think of it as a self-help book that will give you direction and clarity throughout all aspects of the interview process, including what to do leading up to the interview and after the interview. For the rest of your life, whenever you have an interview or are considering a change in position, this book will be your one stop shop to walk you through the entire process.

This book is focused on landing a job in *education,* however, the principles included herein can be applied to almost any industry. The strategies and suggestions made in this book represent a combination of what worked for me and what I have been told by countless other administrators.

My life experiences have given me the opportunity to work in sales, management and then make a career change at age 32 when I entered the world of education as an alternate route teacher of seventh grade math. I have always had a passion for helping others and the path to education felt very natural. Even when I worked in sales (in the private sector), I built positive relationships with my customers and got to know them on a personal level. There was a strong level of trust. I felt incredible satisfaction from learning the challenges of their business and helping to solve their problems. This passion only intensified upon entering the education profession as both a teacher and coach. Teaching and coaching brought me immense satisfaction as it was incredibly rewarding to watch kids grow, learn and improve right in front of your eyes! Now my passion is to share what I have learned. I want to help you find your next job!

My desire to write this book was fueled by my passion to help others. A few years ago, I was asked to offer some advice to an acquaintance. I met her (let's call her *Jane*) for coffee and we talked for about an hour. Jane told me that she hated interviews and would always get very nervous. In less than a week, she had an interview for a school counselor position. She presented as a strong candidate but had minimal experience. School counselor openings are highly coveted and usually attract well over one hundred applicants when there is an opening! Even though she was a strong candidate, she was probably one of fifteen (or so) people who would be interviewing within the next week. I basically gave her the "cliff notes" version of my book. I really enjoyed my conversation with Jane. She listened intently and was fully engaged in our conversation. She was eager to land this position but didn't feel confident in her interviewing skills.

Two weeks later I received a phone call from Jane. I could tell from her tone that she was very excited. She got the job! She thanked me for giving her advice. Jane told me she felt so confident in the interviews (there were actually three in total). I was overwhelmed with satisfaction and was so genuinely happy for her. I knew how important this opportunity was to her. It is that feeling to truly make an impact on others that finally pushed me to write this book.

I didn't get the job for her, as she earned it for herself. All I did was give her a road map that gave her the confidence to relax and let her true self shine through. As you read the chapters ahead, think back to this story.

Once I became an administrator and became the "interviewer" I gained a whole new perspective on the process. I was fortunate to interview and hire some very talented people. However, in recent years, it seems as though the great interviews have become less and less frequent. I have noticed more candidates showing up not prepared; not dressed professionally, walking in empty handed, having no knowledge of my school, and many coming across very casual (almost cavalier in nature). It has become increasingly frustrating to me that many people are not making the most of their opportunity to land a job in education. Being prepared for the interview has become a pet peeve of mine. This source of frustration became a driving motivation to write this book.

It is hard for me to understand since all of the information is out there... just Google it!

How could these candidates come right out of a teaching program (from very reputable institutions of higher learning) and not know how to prepare for an interview? I realized that even though there is a ton of information available, there was a need for a comprehensive book that walked candidates through the entire process from A to Z. I hope this book becomes a great resource for you, one that you will find extremely useful.

You have already heard how I went from alternate route teacher (with no experience) to a high school principal in a short amount of time. I am far from brilliant and there is nothing extraordinary about my skill set.

Then how did it happen? How did I get three promotions within four years and become a high school principal with such limited experience?

There are a few reasons. First, I believe I was very fortunate (you might even say lucky) that there were certain opportunities available to me. Second, I have always prided myself on having a strong work ethic. I have always believed in the value of doing your best. As my father taught me,

"If you are going to do something, you might as well do it right."

Third, and this is an extension of number two, I always made sure I was PREPARED before walking into an interview. Preparation is a theme throughout this book and I cannot stress enough the importance of being 100% prepared for your interview. Dot your I's and cross your T's... Make the most of your opportunity! Keep in mind, it does not take skill to have a strong work ethic and be prepared as *you* have complete control over these two things.

Lastly, I learned the value of being a good communicator when I spent eight years working in sales. The ability to communicate effectively and *connect* with the interviewer was a real difference maker for me. This idea of establishing a rapport with the interviewer, essentially "selling yourself" in the interview is a complex skill that I will delve into deeper later in this book. Bottom line, being able to communicate effectively is an important skill that will enable you to make a positive impression and crush that interview!

I have seen the interview process in education from A to Z from both perspectives... first, as the aspiring administrator climbing the ladder and then on the other side of the table as the *interviewer* (as a principal). I have learned so much from my life experiences, especially in my last eleven years as a principal. I will not hold back anything in the book and I will give you insight into what the interviewer is thinking and expecting from you. I will cover everything from how to land an interview, preparing for your big day (interview), essential interview skills, appropriate follow up, and closing the deal. Let's get started!

Chapter 1
How to Begin Your Job Search

Whether you have decided to begin a career as a teacher, seek a promotion to become an administrator, leave the classroom to become a counselor, or leave private industry (like I did) to become an educator, it is important to have a plan for your job search. In this chapter, I will lay out everything you need to begin your search. Following these steps will greatly help your chances of becoming the successful candidate. Unfortunately, many people ignore the first area that I will cover, networking. I am sure you have heard the old expression,

"It's not what you know but *who* you know."

I do not believe this is an accurate depiction, but I do think networking can open doors that otherwise would remain closed. You never know when you will make a positive impression on someone who is in position to help you get your foot in the door. Interviews are very hard to get, especially for certain positions such as elementary teacher, high school English or history, administrator or guidance counselor. Your goal is to get an interview and get in front of the decision makers!

Networking

Everybody knows someone who works in education. Whether it be as a teacher, counselor or administrator, reach out to the people you know who currently work in the field. Think of your extended family and all of your friends, and make a list of everyone who works in education. Reach out to each person on the list and ask for thirty minutes of their time. If they like coffee, meet them at Starbucks and treat them to their favorite latte. Do whatever it takes, as you want to meet face to face with as many people as reasonably possible. Tell them you are interested in starting a career (or changing careers, like I did) in education and would like some advice on getting into the field. I would also recommend asking about their school. I suggest "asking for *advice* because this is a "non-threatening" approach and most people are willing to talk about themselves and offer their opinions. I learned this approach from a friend named John Corcoran many years ago when I was exploring a career change. John is now a career coach (Corcoran Career Coaching) who also shares my passion for helping others. I will be forever grateful for John taking a personal interest in me and offering his advice. I implore you to follow his approach because it works!

There are two things you want to accomplish at these meetings. First, learn as much as you can about the person's school. Ask about the culture of the school, current initiatives of the school/district, support from administration and their core values. The second (and more important) goal for this meeting is to have the person you are talking to become your supporter, your advocate. If there is an opening in his/her school (or one in the future), you want this person to be confident giving a recommendation to the principal. How do you do this? Start by sharing your passion for helping kids and becoming an educator. As you learn about his/her school, think about how your own life experiences and how they are aligned with this person's school. Share your experiences with this person. Tell them the reasons you are destined to succeed in this profession! Do not go on and on about how great you are; rather, share your passion and rationale in a meaningful, concise manner. For example, if one of the schools' initiatives relates to Social Emotional Learning, share your own experience working with kids as a camp counselor when you helped kids learn slow breathing techniques or when you taught yoga to adults in your gym. You may not have done these things but you get the idea, find a connection with something you have done in your own life.

If one of my staff members offers a recommendation for an applicant, I will immediately take a closer look at his/her resume. In most cases, I will interview the candidate based on the recommendation of a colleague! Of course, every situation is different. For example, if there are an overwhelming number of applicants, I may not interview him/her if they were clearly not as qualified as other candidates. In most circumstances, however, they will get an interview. Think about what I just said…

BASED ON THE RECOMMENDATION OF ONE STAFF MEMBER, YOUR RESUME WILL GET SPECIAL CONSIDERATION THAT WILL LIKELY RESULT IN AN INTERVIEW!

If you were questioning the importance of making the list and setting up those meetings with everyone you know in education, hopefully you're not anymore. Never underestimate the importance or the power of NETWORKING!

When I am reviewing a pile of resumes they have no face, they are simply words on paper. When someone who works in my building, especially someone who is highly respected, recommends a candidate, it matters! It puts a positive face on your resume and enables you to stand out from the competition. At this point, your ONLY GOAL IS TO GET AN INTERVIEW! Interviews are not easy to come by. Make sure you utilize any and all available resources to attain this goal. Don't leave any stone unturned.

Resume

How do you create a resume to stand out in the pile of resumes? I will offer some general guidelines and recommendations. There are many books dedicated to just writing a resume. I thought it was important to include some general suggestions but this is not intended to be everything you need to write a stellar resume.

Your resume is a quick snapshot of your experiences and skill set. It should tell a story of how you can "add value" from the employer's perspective, who will likely only glance at it for 5-10 seconds.

Be concise but descriptive and cite as many relevant experiences as possible. Everything on your resume should be in some way relevant to the position for which you are applying. Nobody cares that you worked at McDonalds during college so do not include it on your resume. Any job where you interacted with kids, however, is relevant. If you were a recreation coach or camp counselor that is worthy of including. These types of experiences can also be great conversation starters!

NEVER lie on a resume. Keep in mind one important thing when writing your resume... You may be asked to elaborate on ANYTHING you write down so make sure you are prepared to do so. You will likely be asked specific questions about what is written and you want to be ready for any question.

Avoid general phrases such as, "Responsible for instructing 100 students." This statement offers no value because it is assumed (as a teacher) that you have a certain number of students for whom you are responsible.

Rather than making a general statement, state something you did to **improve student achievement** or make a positive impact on your students (i.e. created a new program, used a specific teaching strategy, implemented a department initiative, etc.). Highlight what you did or contributed to your school outside the classroom as well (i.e. Coached boys' soccer and created a rewards system for good sportsmanship that resulted in a 50% decrease in yellow/red cards). This approach will help your resume stand out from the others.

I do not presume to be an expert in crafting the perfect resume. There are a million resources online that focus on building a resume. However, I will share some "do's" and "don'ts" that will help your resume stand out in the crowd! These suggestions reflect not only my beliefs but also what colleagues (from other schools) have shared with me.

Let's start by answering an easy question, "How long should my resume be?"

Answer: ONE PAGE

Unless you have more than ten years of relevant experience or have accomplished more than 99% of the population, there is no reason for your resume to exceed one page. The last time I sent out a resume was 2012, with twenty years of work experience, nine in education. My resume was one page. It was sent out in response to an ad for a high school principal. I didn't know anyone in this school district and it was a ninety-minute drive from my home at the time. That one-page piece of paper represented my only opportunity to land an interview. Thankfully, I received a call to come in for an interview. As of this writing, I still work for this district. There's your proof, one page is all you need!

I find it comical when I see a three-page resume from a recent college graduate. Three pages? Really? Keep in mind that the person screening these resumes will be instantly making judgements about you and assessing whether or not you deserve an interview. This person will likely scan your resume for no more than ten seconds, that's it! Cut out the fluff and highlight the MOST IMPORTANT points. Choose quality over quantity. The key is to hit the most important details in a clear, concise manner. This is your chance, your opportunity to demonstrate that you are worthy of an interview. There are a ton of online resources to help build your resume, so use them. Google is free, use it!

There is no magic format to make your resume jump out. However, whichever format you choose should "read easy." Each section of the resume should have the same structure, spacing, font, etc. Ten seconds may be reduced to only four or five seconds if the reader finds it difficult to follow your layout. Use a font that is easy to read and looks professional. DO NOT use any background images or screening on the resume. When in doubt, keep it simple.

What should I include on my resume?

Include any special skills that you possess, extra-curricular areas of interest or expertise and any special recognitions/accomplishments. For example, including that you are a "Google Certified Educator" makes sense, especially if the school district you're applying to uses Google Classroom or other Google products. This will get the reader's attention! Any type of certification or endorsement related to classroom instruction or your expertise using technology should be included. It can also serve as a great conversation starter in the interview.

If you were a college athlete or have experience coaching (on any level) it should be included on your resume. The school may be advertising an opening for an English Teacher but may also need a soccer coach. Your resume will certainly get extra consideration if you can fill both positions.

If you led a service project that had a positive impact on your community, share this information. Maybe the school is looking for an advisor for one of their service clubs. I think you get the idea.

Noting a special recognition that you received is a great conversation piece (and should be included on your resume) during an interview. This topic will be discussed later when we focus on *connecting with the interviewer.*

Now let's turn our focus to the meat and potatoes of the resume. The body of your resume will focus on relevant work experience. The toughest part of writing a dynamic resume is deciding exactly *what to write* about each job experience. Choose your words carefully and focus on what you are most PROUD OF. As noted earlier, avoid listing general responsibilities that are assumed as part of the job. Answer the question,

"How did you add value or make a difference?"

If you are describing your student teaching experience, you *do not* need a bullet to state that you taught eighth grade math to ninety students. Rather, focus on what you did to improve student learning for those ninety students (i.e. implemented a new digital learning program that increased student achievement by more than 20%). I would suggest having 3-4 bullets under each job experience.

Some questions to consider…

> Have you led any school initiatives from start to finish?
> Have you turn-keyed or presented an instructional tool or strategy to your colleagues?

Have you implemented an "outside the box" teaching strategy that had a profound impact on student learning?
Was there a memorable moment during your student teaching that is worth including?

These are the types of bullet points to include on your resume. They are ATTENTION GRABBERS!! You have one page of information to make an impression on the person reading your resume. Think about how you will stand out. Your bullet points should be well-written statements that focus on your accomplishments or the accomplishments of your students.

People often ask, "Should I include references on my resume?"

Before schools went to online applications, I would have suggested either listing your references on your resume or simply stating, "References available upon request." However, since it is likely that you will be asked to list your references on your application, there is no need to list them on your resume. Remember, you want that resume to be as streamlined as possible.

Cover Letter

This is your opportunity to show off your writing skills in a clear, concise manner. As far as the content of your letter, focus on the skills that set you apart from the competition. This is an opportunity to stand out in the pile of applicants. Whoever is reading this cover letter is making judgements about your intelligence and writing ability. Make sure your grammar is perfect. Have multiple people (including at least one English teacher) read and review your cover letter.

How long should it be?

There is no magic answer here but I will offer some guidance. Half a page is too short as the interviewer is likely to think you don't have much to say. A page and a half is too long and will give the impression that you can't get to the point! I suggest at least three-quarters of a page, but not more than one full page.

One more thing about the cover letter, and this is important... BE TRANSPARENT! If your resume has a gap in employment, use your cover letter to explain *why* there is a gap. If you are applying for a job in New York but live in Pennsylvania, state that you intend to relocate if you are the successful candidate. If you were formerly a supervisor and now work as a teacher, explain *why* you went back to being a teacher. The point is that many people have these "holes" or 'question marks' on their resume that can raise a red flag with the interviewer.

Don't get put in the "NO" pile because of a *RED FLAG*! Be open, tell your story, and be transparent. People will respect your honesty and you will gain credibility. Use the cover letter to share your story and sell yourself. Make sure it is well written, grammatically correct and accurately conveys your passion to help kids succeed.

Completing the Application

Almost every school will have some form of an online application. After all, it is 2020! Gone are the days of sending out a bunch of resumes via snail mail. It is likely that the application will require you to upload certain documents such as a resume, certifications and college transcript. Some of the other information you will need to type in. Let me stop here to give you a critical warning… DO NOT ASSUME THAT THE DOCUMENT YOU UPLOAD WILL LOOK IDENTICAL ON THE OTHER SIDE. Depending on the formatting and the program being used by the school district, the document may be altered. Therefore, refrain from using any fancy markings or background logos on any document that you upload. I have received several documents that had either a faded logo in the background or a colored picture that prevented me from viewing the content of the document. Guess what happened to those applications? They were discarded! One other piece of advice, use PDF files. Word files sometimes get altered but a PDF will not. One silly error on your part can be catastrophic so *PLEASE* do not alter any of your documents or try to make them look fancy. Keep it simple!

There will be questions for you to answer on the application. My first word of advice is to BE HONEST! It may seem obvious but it is critical that you are transparent and honest throughout the entire process, and that starts with the application. For example, there may be a question such as, "Have you ever been placed on leave by your employer?" There may have been a situation where you were put on leave for being falsely accused of some wrongdoing. When coming across this question, many people will be tempted to lie and not admit to this in fear of their application being discarded, especially if they didn't even do anything wrong. Do not fall into this trap! Be transparent and answer the question honestly. You will most likely be asked to explain the situation. When doing so, state the facts and be concise with your response. And remember, it is 2020 and there is no such thing as a secret. The Internet and Google searches have forever changed the concept of privacy. It is much better for the potential employer to hear this information from you.

On the application, you will likely be asked to list 3-5 references. Ideally, you have an excellent relationship with both your immediate supervisor and building principal. If so, definitely include them as references. A mentor or other colleague would be a suitable third choice. Do not be shy about using references from other school districts. Maybe you worked on a county-wide curriculum committee and hit it off with a curriculum director from another district. Think back to networking.

Reach out to her or him and tell them how much you enjoyed working with them on the committee. Tell them about your situation and that you are seeking a new opportunity. Ask them for their permission to be listed as a reference. You never know how important this call could be. Hopefully they will give you permission to list them as a reference (most people will be flattered and agree to be a reference). Best case scenario, this person shares that they have a retirement coming up mid-year in their district and suggests that you apply. The point is to get your name out there! Once you have a solid list of three references, now think of friends in reputable positions to list as fourth or fifth references.

What if you aren't employed by a school? Who do you use as references?

Hopefully you were networking and building relationships during your student teaching experience. Your teacher mentor and any administrator who observed you would be a good place to start. While student teaching, I strongly recommend asking an administrator to observe you and give you feedback. I would also recommend getting to know as many teachers and administrators as possible. Don't be shy about asking multiple people to observe you in the classroom. Even if they can only stay 10-15 minutes, you have an opportunity to impress them. You never know if there will be an opportunity in that school. Maybe your teaching skills and desire to learn will be the difference in them offering you an opportunity. Doing the little things will help you stand out from others.

Every student teacher is assigned an advisor from their college program. He/she should also be listed as a reference. This person will get to know you well and it's important that you cultivate this relationship. This person should have no doubts about your passion for teaching, your work ethic and commitment to learn/grow

Deciding where to apply

You have made every effort to elicit help from others (by networking), you have mastered the best approach for completing an application, and you have crafted a well-written cover letter and resume. You are now ready to start applying to schools!

Begin searching online and find the best sites for jobs in education (varies by state). Whether you are right out of a college teaching program or switching careers, I recommend applying <u>everywhere</u> within a reasonable distance. It is up to you to decide how far you are willing to commute. Obviously, the larger the geographical area, the more schools you have to choose from, and this will increase your chances of finding a suitable match. If you are currently a teacher, and seeking a new position as a counselor or administrator, I would strongly recommend expanding your search to as many schools as possible, as these positions tend to have fewer openings and are usually harder to secure.

There are many variables to consider (when deciding where to apply) that are different for each person. Some questions to consider that will impact how far you are willing to commute and how selective you will be when applying may include the following:

> What is my financial situation?
> Do I *need* to begin working ASAP, or can I take my time to find a position?
> Are there external factors to consider such as kids, spouse, or other responsibilities in my life?

Spend some time reflecting on the questions above and be honest with yourself. Only you can determine how quickly you need to find a job and how far you are willing to commute.

The reason I suggest applying to as many places as possible is two-fold. First, finding a job is a numbers game. The more lines you have in the water, the better chance you have of catching a fish! The second reason is equally important. The more places you apply, the more likely you are to go on multiple interviews.

One of the themes in this book is the importance of preparation. I will go into great detail later about preparing for your big day, the actual interview. However, there is no better preparation for being successful in an interview than PRACTICE. Even if you get a call from a district that does not interest you, I suggest accepting the interview and preparing as if you are interviewing for your dream job. The experience of preparing for the interview, sitting through the interview and then receiving feedback after the interview, will be invaluable!

Another thing to consider… you may *think* you have no interest in this school, but after going through the process, your opinion may change. Maybe you are blown away with the people you meet in the interview or maybe you learn that the school is taking on a new initiative that aligns with your belief system. Bottom line, you will never know for sure until you go through the process. Worst case scenario, it was great practice and you just became more skilled at the interview process.

For those of you who don't *need* a new job, you are in a very desirable position. There is no pressure to be perfect in the interview. It is a completely different dynamic that should allow you to relax and let your true personality shine. Think back to my situation in Hawthorne. I was an assistant principal and loved my school and the person I was working for. I didn't *need* a new job. This is actually the best time to explore other opportunities. This may seem counterintuitive.

Why would I look for a new job when I am happy in my current position?

If your ultimate goal is to take on a new role, then you need to be open to the idea of finding a new "home." This is a great position to be in because there is no pressure to apply everywhere (as would be the case if you need a new job). Remember, I only applied to two High School Principal openings because those were the only two jobs that appealed to me. Secondly, if you are offered a position, there is no pressure to jump at the opportunity. It has to be the right situation for you. If something doesn't feel right you can simply walk away knowing that you are happy in your current position. I declined my first offer to become a high school principal because I didn't think it was the right fit for me. I decided I would rather remain an assistant principal in Hawthorne than accept the offer that was presented to me. When you are content with your current situation, it allows you to be in control of your own decisions. Finally, being happy where you are changes the dynamics of the interview process. You are interviewing your potential employer just as much as they are interviewing you. Psychologically, you are on a level playing field, with both sides trying to determine if the other is the right fit. This dynamic is completely different from an interview when you _need_ the job because you are either unemployed or miserable in your current position.

One word of caution when in the position of not *needing* a new job. DO NOT come across as arrogant. I know you don't need the job, but they shouldn't. Be confident and relaxed, but coming across as too confident can easily turn off the people sitting across from you. Options are a great thing and you want to have as many as possible. There is no reason to eliminate an opportunity because you are not in the right mindset. Relax, be yourself and put your best foot forward!

I encourage you to be aggressive in your search. I'm not suggesting to become a pest and constantly call the schools to which you have applied. However, there is nothing wrong with a phone call one week after you've completed an application to confirm that they received your application. In doing so, take the opportunity to express that you are still very interested in the position. There are various factors that may affect how aggressive you are, including your own comfort level.

Think back to my Roy Brown story, when I landed my first teaching job. That would have never happened if I hadn't made the bold decision to show up and ask the principal to give me five minutes of his time. I'm not suggesting that you need to go to that extreme, as every situation is different. That was late August, and I knew the school was just as desperate to fill the position as I was to find one. Also, my personality suggests that I am not averse to taking a risk, when the situation presents itself. When you are faced with a dilemma and are contemplating a bold move, consider the pros and cons of the situation. In my case, I knew the worst-case scenario was the principal refusing to meet with me and I would have embarked on a fifteen-minute ride for nothing. The worst-case scenario was wasting thirty minutes of my day and being in the exact same place I was... unemployed. The best-case scenario would be meeting with the principal, winning him over, and then being offered a job. In my mind, this was a "no-brainer" because I really had nothing to lose. You need to be comfortable in your approach. Maybe you are a little more reserved and would not be comfortable making a bold move. That's ok. Keep in mind that following up, however, is usually appreciated by an employer.

A word of advice when applying for open positions, do it ASAP! Don't make the mistake of looking at the end date for the posting and putting off your application. I can tell you first hand that most of the time the interviews begin before the posting closes and if there are several high-quality candidates that emerge, the applications that come in late may not even be considered! Get your application in as soon as possible as it will only help your chances of getting an interview.

Create a portfolio

Is it really necessary to create a portfolio?

You're damn right it is! Creating a comprehensive portfolio is one way to set yourself apart from the competition. First off, when you show up for an interview with an impressive collection of documents/artifacts contained within a portfolio it screams,

"I am a professional, detail-oriented person who is ready to impress you!"

There is no better way to start an interview than making a great first impression. Secondly, there might be an opportunity (during the interview) for you to refer to a document in the portfolio to better illustrate a point. Lastly, leaving a portfolio behind with the interviewer ensures that you have a tangible document for them to read and learn more about you. Even though you're not *physically* in front of them, your name is still in front of them.

Your portfolio should include the following documents/artifacts:
- Educational philosophy
- Resume
- Letters of recommendation (at least three)
- Exemplary lesson plans (at least three)
- Samples of student work (at least three)
- Miscellaneous artifacts that speak to your excellence as an educator (i.e. exceedingly positive email from a parent or former student)

*The size of your portfolio will depend on how many years you have worked in education.

Professionalism & Social Media

It is important to conduct yourself as a professional at all times in any industry, and education is no different. I would argue that qualities such as professionalism, integrity and character are even more important in the education arena because you are dealing directly with children. Administrators are not looking for teachers to become "friends" with students; they are looking for positive role models who will have an overtly positive impact on students. From the very first interaction with the school staff and throughout the interview process, always carry yourself with professionalism and demonstrate a high level of integrity. It doesn't matter how talented you are or what an amazing teacher you may be, lacking in this area will undoubtedly derail your chances of becoming the chosen candidate.

At the writing of this book, it is 2020 and social media has become a huge piece of American culture. I want to share a word of caution… be mindful of what you post or say on social media! Remember, anything said on social media is there for EVERYONE to see! Before making a post, ask yourself a very important question…

"If my potential employer read this comment right now, would it negatively impact me in any way?"

This is the essential question that you must consider before writing something that could be offensive or come across as unprofessional. I will share a story about an acquaintance who learned a hard lesson about social media. He was interviewing for his dream job as a teacher and coach in a school district. He was well-prepared for the interview process and made a great impression. The district was ready to hire him before they found a post on Instagram that they deemed to be unprofessional. They decided to go with another candidate and this young man had learned a very valuable lesson.

Many districts will look up your social media accounts. I suggest keeping your profile private and not engaging in anything controversial. I do believe that everyone is entitled to a private life; however, social media has forever changed how others have access into your life. It is important to remember that when it comes to education, employers are seeking high quality people who they can trust to be role models for children. This is an incredible responsibility and employers want to know they are hiring people of integrity and high moral fiber. When on social media, think before to speak and never lose out on an opportunity because of a foolish post.

Chapter 2
You Landed an Interview... Now What?

Preparation is the key to your success! Even the most confident and skilled person will perform significantly better if they are 100% prepared. My father believed in a simple formula that applied to life, and it is definitely relevant here. He didn't believe that luck was a product of chance, but luck as being defined as *when preparation meets opportunity*. This is your opportunity, so make the most of it!

The single, most common reason people fail in an interview is nerves. I have seen it time and time again. I can recall several occasions when a supervisor had met with a candidate and raved about how amazing the candidate was, and then they bombed the second interview with me.

Why did this happen? Did their personality change in 48 hours? Did they become less intelligent? Obviously, the answer to both questions is no, so what happened?

Nerves got the best of them. Being thoroughly prepared will settle your nerves and allow you to thrive in the interview.

All of the steps I recommend in this chapter are centered around preparing you to put your best foot forward in the interview. Be diligent and thorough as you complete the action steps I have laid out.

Do your homework

This is where things really start to get exciting. In my opinion, the hardest part of the entire interview process is landing an interview. Now that you have successfully attained this goal, you can focus your attention on learning about the school and preparing for your big day. I cannot stress enough the importance of researching the school before your interview. There is nothing more annoying to a principal than a candidate who makes a general statement such as, "I've heard great things about your school," yet they actually know NOTHING about the school.

There is a ton of information on a school's website. You have access to general information about the school, test scores, curriculum, schedule, goals, educational philosophy, you name it. And the best part, all of this valuable information is FREE! Read it, study it, and get to know the school and what they *value*. Doing research will also help you come up with meaningful questions for you to ask during the interview. Asking well-crafted questions based on your knowledge of a school will leave a lasting impression on the interviewers.

Focus on the goals of the school and the district. Some questions to research include:

What are the key initiatives the school is focused on?
What is their professional development plan for staff?
What is the reading/writing program at the primary grades?
What math program is being utilized in the elementary schools?
What is the high school graduation rate?
What percentage of graduates are attending four-year colleges?
How much value does the school place on extra-curricular activities such as athletics, performing arts and service clubs?

Answers to the questions above will give you valuable insight into the school. You can also expect to get asked a question or two about one of their initiatives or goals. You will definitely impress the interviewer if you have knowledge on this topic and are able to construct an educated response. If there is not a question about a school initiative, which is unlikely, then *you* have an ideal opportunity to ask a question at the end of the interview (more on *asking questions* later).

Do your homework on the school and if you come across an initiative that you are not familiar with LEARN ABOUT IT! You probably know other people in education you can ask OR simply Google it. Remember, knowledge is a powerful tool!

List your biggest accomplishments

Now that you have become familiar with the school that you're interviewing with; your next step is to write down your biggest accomplishments. These are the ones you are most proud of and bring a big smile to your face. Not all of them must be related to education, but most of them should be. These accomplishments may be used as talking points during your interview or you may end up referring to them when answering a specific question. Read them over several times and know them inside out. They should tell a story about your ability to lead a process from start to finish, accomplish something extraordinary or demonstrate how your work ethic allowed you to overcome a major obstacle. Spend some time brainstorming your accomplishments and the "stories" that accompany them. Lastly, think about possible questions you may be asked after sharing one or more of these accomplishments. Consider the following questions:

- What obstacles did you face along the way?
- How did you handle these obstacles?
- Why do you think you were successful?
- How did you get colleagues involved?
- Was there any resistance from colleagues?

- How did you attempt to get 'buy in' from naysayers?
- What did you learn during the process?
- If you faced the same challenge again, what would you do differently?

Review your portfolio

The next step in preparing for your big day is to review your portfolio. Your portfolio has already been created and is ready to go. Read through it carefully to make sure there aren't any errors or irrelevant documents. I am not suggesting that you need a different portfolio for each school you interview at; however, there may be a few tweaks from one interview to another. For example, when doing research, you learned that School X places a strong emphasis on technology. When going through your portfolio, you decide to add a lesson plan that incorporates several aspects of using technology in the classroom. This lesson was strong, but didn't make your initial top three list so it wasn't included when you originally compiled the documents for your portfolio. Make sure you reflect on what you learned about School X and add any relevant documents to your portfolio.

Now that you have researched the school, made your list of accomplishments and reviewed your portfolio, it is time to focus on preparing for possible interview questions.

Possible interview questions

It is now time to begin preparing for the questions you may be asked during the interview. I will offer some examples but this is not an exhaustive list. Remember, it is very simple to search "interview questions" for a teacher, counselor or school administrator. With that said, there are some standard questions that you should be able to ace in your interview.

"Tell me about yourself and why you are interested in this position."

This is one of the most common openings to an interview. Unfortunately, for many applicants, this simple question can be catastrophic if you don't have a plan. Some candidates will use this open-ended question as an opportunity to ramble on and on about themselves. Many times, people will go off on tangents and bring up their childhood, previous careers, or hobbies. Let me give you one piece of advice...STAY FOCUSED AND GET TO THE POINT! I am not suggesting to rush your answer, but everything you say should be connected (at least in some way) to why you are applying for this position and why you will be an exceptional hire. It's hard for me to say exactly how long your response should be, but one to two minutes sounds about right.

Let's review some common questions and analyze sample responses.

Question: *Why are you looking to make the change from teacher to school counselor?*

Sample response: "I've been teaching for ten years and realized that my true calling is to help kids as a counselor. I have always enjoyed helping my students resolve conflicts and think about their future. I completed my internship in the spring and started looking for counselor openings. I saw that you had an opening here and decided to apply."

This response is definitely too brief and more importantly, lacks substance. When answering any question in an interview, think about the *value* you bring to the table.

Why did you decide to become a counselor?
Was there a driving force or motivation that led to this decision?
What qualities do you possess that make you confident you will be an effective counselor?
Do you have any practical examples of when you demonstrated the ability to help a student through a difficult situation?
Do you have any experience using conflict resolution strategies?

Give some thought to the questions above and apply them to your situation. If you are an aspiring counselor, take 10-15 minutes and write out responses to these questions. This exercise will help you organize your thoughts and focus on the value that you bring to the table. This exercise can also be applied to an aspiring teacher who is possibly fresh out of school or changing careers from another industry. Think about your life experiences and how they relate to being successful in the job for which you are applying!

Consider an alternative response to the question above about your desire to become a school counselor...

"I have been teaching for ten years now and absolutely love going to work every day. I believe two of my greatest strengths as a teacher are connecting with my students and motivating them to be successful (provide one example to support each area of strength). I am passionate about mentoring students and helping them reach their potential. I finished my counseling internship in the spring and absolutely loved the experience of helping kids every day. I was researching your school and noticed that one of your district goals is incorporating *mindfulness* in the classroom. I have implemented mindful tips/tools with my students and believe they have reaped tremendous benefits from these activities (Briefly explain *how* students benefited). I was able to take what I had done in the classroom and use this approach in my counseling internship. One of my school's goals was centered around Social Emotional Learning. I volunteered to train teachers who didn't have experience using mindfulness in the classroom."

Hopefully the difference between these two responses is obvious. The second response is longer, but more importantly, it contains plenty of substance! There are specific examples to support your claims, and they are relevant to the position. There is also a willingness to help others to advance a goal of the building, all in one paragraph! Everything in the second response is directly connected to why you are making the change to school counselor AND also provides a rationale for why you will be successful in this role. As an added benefit, it also demonstrates a strong work ethic and a willingness to be a team player.

Now let's look at a common question in a teacher interview.

"Give me a feel for your teaching style. Tell me how you structure a typical lesson in your classroom; and in doing so, break down the lesson into pieces (beginning, middle and end)."

Consider the following approach:
Start with an overview of how you would break down a lesson. Begin with some type of a *hook* to pique students' interest; then, transition to either a brief period of direct instruction or a technology-enhanced learning activity, followed by group work where students will work together (collaborate) to either solve a problem or discuss/debate a topic; finally, the lesson will conclude with a closure activity to assess student comprehension.

There may be some minor adjustments to your "typical" lesson but that is a good starting point. Most importantly, make sure there is a logical progression of activities from beginning to end.

As you elaborate on your answer, always keep *assessment* in mind. Describe what you and the students are doing at various times during the lesson. For example, as you are circulating the room and listening to the group discussions, state that you will be checking for accuracy but also looking for opportunities to enrich/extend learning. For example, if one group demonstrates a strong grasp of a skill, you might ask a thought-provoking question to further challenge these students. For groups that master the activity quickly, explain how you will challenge them and keep them engaged. Conversely, for those groups that struggle, have some *guiding hints* prepared to assist them. In addition, consider other strategies to break down complex concepts/questions into smaller pieces that are easier to understand.

How do you know your students are meeting the objectives of the lesson?

When addressing this question, focus on the *evidence* of student learning. Whether it be some form of assessment completed by the students or some other quantitative measure, it is important to convey proof of understanding. Listening to student conversations may give you an idea of how students are grasping the concepts as a group but the real measure of student outcomes is demonstrated by what the students can produce.

When planning a lesson, teachers should always ask themselves,

"How will I know if my students are understanding the key points of the lesson?"

Think back to walking around the room while students are working in groups. The questions you ask and the feedback you receive are important clues as to how well students are grasping the content. During this process, take it a step further and *document* your observations. Keep notes on the progress of different groups (and individual students). It doesn't matter if you use an electronic device or pen and paper, but make sure to take detailed notes about your students' progress. This data will later be used to inform your planning on the subsequent lesson(s). Common follow up questions to your response to the question above will likely be one or both of the following:

"What will you do with the student data you collect?"
"How will it inform your instruction moving forward?"

Think about what you will do with this data. For example, maybe pairing struggling learners with more advanced students is the appropriate strategy; or maybe there is only a handful of struggling learners so you decide to have them complete a different task (than the rest of the class) to reinforce the main concept. Every situation is different and there are many factors to consider including learning styles, personalities and the overall dynamics of the class. I strongly suggest educating yourself on all aspects of *assessment* as it is a topic that will undoubtedly come up in every interview!

Here are a few other teacher-related questions that you should be prepared to answer:

Q: How do you build a good rapport with your students?

Focus on creating a culture of respect in your classroom; respect as a two-way street; getting to know your students' interests outside the classroom; attending student events such as games, plays, concerts, ceremonies, recognitions, etc.

Q: What is your approach to classroom management?

Start with *respect* again; treating all students fairly; rules and procedures that students have a say in establishing; consistent follow through of rules; strong communication with students and parents; praise students regularly and have a systematic approach for making *positive* phone calls to parents. **Parents love hearing from a teacher when their child is doing well!** Establishing a positive connection with a parent can prove highly beneficial when you need to have a more difficult conversation in the future, such as if the child is not doing well in class.

Q: How do you differentiate learning to ensure all students are successful in your class?

Every lesson should be designed with two things in mind… students have different learning styles AND not all students have the same ability level; therefore, they will not learn at the same pace. With this in mind, every lesson should incorporate different approaches to learning; for example, collaboration in groups for the social learner, videos/visual depictions for the more visual learner and something to get kids out of their seats and moving (i.e. jigsaw activity) for the kinesthetic learner. In addition, assignments should be tiered to varying levels of difficulty in order to appropriately challenge every student in the class. All students should be working on the same skills, however, vocabulary may be modified or guiding hints (such as steps to solve a problem) may be provided to help struggling students. Some students will benefit from breaking down big ideas into smaller pieces that are easier to comprehend, commonly known as "chunking" a lesson.

The Night Before

1. Review your list of accomplishments to have these potential talking points on the tip of your tongue.

2. Prepare your interview folder with a pad (inside insert) and a nice pen. The folder should also contain your list of accomplishments (discussed earlier) and questions that you intend to ask (to be discussed later). You should bring extra copies of your resume. You will also take your portfolio to the interview (spiral bound book or some other professional looking cover).

3. Write out possible interview questions. What do you think they will ask? Think about what responses you will offer to these questions. Going through this simple exercise will put you in the right frame of mind and help you avoid the dreaded "drawing a blank" moment.

4. Remind yourself that you are 100% prepared for your big day tomorrow. You are prepared, confident, and ready to have a great interview. Knowing that you are prepared will enable you to relax and hopefully get some sleep!

5. Pick out your clothes the night before - make sure your best suit is dry cleaned and ready to go.

6. Set your alarm to wake up early.

Chapter 3
Gameday

Today is your big day. It is time to get your brain mentally prepared. Start by waking up early and leave plenty of time to have a healthy breakfast. I would also suggest spending twenty minutes doing something to center yourself and get in a positive state of mind. Depending on your preference, pick one of the following activities… go for a run, lift weights, yoga, meditate or listen to a motivational video. If you are feeling really ambitious, pick two activities! In a short while, you will be in your car beaming with confidence and energy.

Arrival at the interview

Now that you are in the right mindset, you are ready to embrace your big moment. Plan on arriving ten minutes early for the interview. If you get there twenty minutes early, sit in your car until ten minutes before your scheduled interview time. You want to be early, but not too early. Do not be late! Leave yourself extra time in case of traffic or if you get lost. The last thing you need is added stress because you are rushing to get there on time. Plan ahead and get there early.

Dress like a professional. I have seen countless candidates show up in casual clothes looking like they had just rolled out of bed. You can do all of the research and preparation I suggested, however, if you are not dressed professionally you will sabotage your interview before it even begins! Regardless of the position for which you are applying, wear a suit. This is an absolute must. You want to look your best so clothes should be ironed, shoes polished and make sure to be well groomed. Do not wear anything that could be construed as inappropriate. You are interviewing for a job, not going out on the town. I believe in the old adage... look good, feel good, play good! You are about to partake in one of the most important *games* of your life, make sure this is reflected in your appearance. Bringing a portfolio, arriving on time and being dressed for success will not automatically land you the job, but not doing so can most certainly cost you an opportunity.

When arriving for your interview, be courteous to everyone you encounter, especially the secretaries! Try to engage them in conversation. You never know, you might even gain a little insight about the position. After *every* interview, I ask my secretary about the candidate.

What was their demeanor when they arrived? Were they friendly? What were they doing while they waited for the interview to begin?

That is correct, the person who *greets* you will be giving critical input to the decision-maker!

When you arrive, look for a school paper or anything that has information about the school. Maybe you will learn something new that will be a topic of conversation in the interview. You never know. Look around the office and take note of what you see.

There is nothing more frustrating to me than when a candidate shows up for an interview empty handed. Really? You are about to spend the next 45-60 minutes interviewing for a job that is a potentially life-changing opportunity and you bring nothing? EVERY applicant, even if you are fresh out of college, should have a portfolio. Whether you have lesson plans from student teaching or documented success stories from your internship as a school counselor, bring your portfolio to the interview, and SHARE IT WITH THE INTERVIEWER! The portfolio should be organized neatly in a binder and highlight the skills and experiences that set you apart from the other applicants.

Sell Yourself

I recall one of the first lessons I learned in my first job out of college (a sales position with Standard Register). The lesson was simple and very true… *people buy from people they like!* The same concept is applicable to

interviews. **People want to hire people they like.** The most common question a boss (in any industry) will ask the interviewer, *"Did you like the candidate?"*
If there is a teacher vacancy with a lot of candidates it is not uncommon for a supervisor to do the first round of interviews. When this happens, what question will the principal ask the supervisor?

"How many candidates did you like?"

I don't want to get too much into the emotional motivations of why people hire a candidate but I do want to stress the importance of *likeability*. The interviewer(s) will be forming opinions of you from the second you enter the room; factors such as eye contact, facial expressions, handshake and your appearance will all play a critical role in making that first impression. Walk in with a smile on your face, dressed to impress and offer a friendly but firm handshake while looking directly at the person and say,

"It is a pleasure to meet you." You are off to a good start!

When there is an opportunity to talk about one of your accomplishments, take it. Share your passion! You have a portfolio with you so use it. Don't just bring it with you, share it with the interviewer. When you are asked about planning a lesson, open up the portfolio and show him/her an example of what you have done. Answering a question with words is fine but showing a visual representation of how you implemented a strategy in the classroom will leave a lasting impression! Using your portfolio to support your answers can be a game changer. This is your chance to stand out and demonstrate why *YOU* are the best choice. Show up prepared, and use every resource possible to make a strong impression. It is so unfortunate that many candidates show up empty handed. Don't ever be one of those people.

If you are interviewing to be a school counselor and are asked about setting up small group counseling sessions, open up your portfolio and share the outline from the "group sessions" that you led during your internship. Speak to each document and share how your plan made a positive impact on students.

If you're interviewing for an assistant principal position, share how your classroom management approach positively impacted student behavior or how you had success using positive behavior supports in your classroom. Maybe you collected data to show how you reduced discipline referrals by implementing specific strategies. Maybe you tracked positive phone calls to parents and found a correlation to increased student outcomes. Think of your success stories in your current position and the skills that led to these positive outcomes.

Ask yourself, "*Are these skills transferable to the position for which you are applying?*"

Even though I became an administrator after only three years in the classroom, I was able to succeed because of the transferable skills I had acquired from working in the private sector.

Connecting with the interviewer

Connecting with a complete stranger is not easy. For many people, it is the hardest part of the interview. You can study a list of possible questions and become well-versed in instructional strategies, classroom management, technology, assessment, etc. However, connecting with an interviewer on a personal level is hard! You have a limited amount of time to win this person over and convince them that you will be a great asset to his/her school.

How do you connect with the interviewer?

Step 1: Likeability

First and foremost, you want the interviewer to view you as likeable. We just reviewed the opening of the interview so hopefully you are off to a good start. What you say and do will influence the interviewer's opinion of you. Use positive words and demonstrate enthusiasm. The interviewer is also trying to determine how well you will fit into his/her school. It may seem obvious, but being positive, friendly and enthusiastic about this opportunity are absolutely imperative!

Step 2: Do your homework on the person interviewing you

Leading up to the interview, you should have read up on the interviewer, and know their background, interests, career path, etc. At some point during the interview you will have an opportunity to connect with the interviewer on a personal level. Maybe you searched Google and learned they wrote a book that was of interest to you, maybe you found them on social media and learned they share a similar hobby with you, or maybe they used to work in a school district that was very similar to where you did your student teaching, etc. Don't force it but be mindful of an opportunity to bring up a common point of interest, especially if it is relevant to the conversation.

Step 3: Share a success story

When an opportunity presents itself to talk about one of the accomplishments on your list, share your story! If a question arises that is relevant to one of your accomplishments, use this opportunity to share the story of your success. Take advantage of this opportunity to share how you did something special.

Step 4: Relax and be yourself

I want to emphasize that *knowledge is power*. The more you know, the more confident you will be, and the more confident you are, the more relaxed you will be in the interview. Once you are relaxed, your true personality will come through. You want to be professional, maintain good eye contact, connect with the interviewer, but most importantly, you want to BE YOURSELF! One of the most important questions I ask myself when considering a candidate is,

"Will he/she be able to connect with our students?"

If you come across as stiff or too rigid, the answer will be NO. **Professional but relatable** is what you are shooting for! Regardless of the position you are applying for in education, you must be able to connect with and relate to kids! This quality is an absolute must.

What to do if stumped by a question

We have all been in this situation at some point in our career. It can be unnerving when you are asked a question and your brain has no answer. I remember when this happened to me. It feels like it was yesterday, although it was actually more than fourteen years ago! I thought the interview was going well and BAM... it happened. I was asked to name the last educational book I had read. Seems simple enough. After all, I had recently completed my masters in educational leadership and had read several books on education. Unfortunately for me, at that moment, I could not recall a single book title or author.

If this happens, the first thing to do is remain calm. Take a breath and think about the substance of the question. There are one of two reasons you are drawing a blank. Either you can't remember something in that moment (like me) OR you simply don't have knowledge of the topic.

Scenario 1 - Cannot recall information
Be patient and it will likely come to you. There is nothing wrong with an honest response such as, "I cannot recall at this moment; however, I can tell you...." Proceed to share what you know related to the topic. Once you start talking, it is likely you will recall the information that was escaping your brain.

Scenario 2 - No knowledge of the topic
Hopefully with all of your preparation, this will not happen. However, in case it does, you need a plan. Rather than offer an incorrect answer that may come across as disingenuous, I suggest taking the honest approach. Take a negative and turn it into a positive. Here is an example...

"Honestly, I am not familiar with that teaching strategy but I will be sure to learn about it tonight."

Ok, so you didn't know the answer; however, with one sentence you just conveyed that you are honest, eager to learn and willing to act when you don't know something! That doesn't sound so bad to me. The best part, however, will come in the *thank you letter.* Once you do your research on this topic, you will comment on what you learned in your thank you letter (to be discussed later).

Share your passion

First and foremost, make sure to emphasize your passion for working with kids and making a difference in their lives. After all, this should be one of the driving reasons you want to work in education! Demonstrate a commitment to your belief system but ALWAYS include self-growth and professional development. Emphasize your EAGERNESS to continue learning and seek professional development (PD) opportunities. You need to speak their language. Education has become all about incorporating new technologies, innovative pedagogical approaches and personalized learning. Every administrator is looking for a candidate who will embrace PD and personal growth.

Do not be afraid to bring up an area of passion, whether it be using technology in the classroom or mastering the most recent research on differentiating instruction. If you learned a new approach or strategy and then implemented it in your classroom, share this in your interview. Hopefully you had the opportunity to invite supervisors and other administrators into your classroom and get their input. This will undoubtedly make a great impression on the interviewer.

Now take it to the next level… Share your vision for mastering this initiative and then offer to turnkey it to other staff at a department or faculty meeting. Wow! You are not only looking to become a difference maker for your students but also make a difference schoolwide! You do not need to be a 20-year veteran teacher to be a leader. Principals are looking to hire WINNERS, LEADERS, and people who will be great teachers but also make a positive impact on the entire school. Do not leave any doubt that you are a person who takes action, craves learning and is a leader among peers.

If this is an interview for a position as an administrator, collaboration is a central theme for achieving success on many levels. Share your vision for shared decision making and including all stakeholders in major decisions. In your preparation, you will establish a clear vision for your leadership style but including teachers, students and parents in major decisions is a sound practice.

Here is an example of how shared decision making can prove to be a successful strategy...

During my first year as a principal, I asked a ton of questions, learned how the school functioned (what worked well and what needed improvement) and started developing positive relationships with my staff. I also started a Principal's Committee composed of students from different grade levels. I wanted to learn as much as I could and get input from all stakeholders, including students. I did not make any changes in my first year as I wanted to gain a strong understanding of the culture and needs of the school. After my first year, I learned that we were in desperate need of a new Attendance Policy. In year two, I formed a committee of administrators, teachers, counselors, parents and students. A policy change such as this affects everyone, therefore, I felt it was important to get input and buy in from each group. I wanted to ensure that we addressed the concerns of all parties. This process can be applied to any number of situations an administrator may encounter. Creating committees to allow for multiple perspectives from various stakeholder groups is an example of why *collaboration* is an essential component of effective leadership.

What questions should I ask?

You have responded to several questions over the past 45-60 minutes as the interview is nearing the end. Hopefully you were able to connect with the interviewer(s), share some of your accomplishments and make a strong first impression. Now it is time to respond to one last question…

"Do you have any questions for us?"

I recommend having three questions planned (written down on the pad inside your folder) and ready to go. You may not ask all three but be prepared to do so if the situation calls for it. More about that decision in a minute...

These questions should be based on your research of the school/district. Closely examine the goals of the school (on their website). One question should be based on one of these goals. Consider the following two examples.

"I read that one of your goals this year is focused on mental health. I am very interested in this initiative and have studied different approaches to social-emotional learning. I implemented mindfulness activities in my classroom. Is this an initiative that will continue to be an area of focus moving forward? If so, would I have an opportunity to contribute in some way? I would be willing to train other teachers in mindful practices, if needed."

"I was reading about your school and I learned that you have a one-to-one Chromebook initiative set to begin in September. Is there a committee in place leading this change? If so, would there be an opportunity for a new teacher who is highly skilled using technology to assist in any way?"

These questions/explanations say a few things to the interviewer. First, he/she will know you researched the school. Secondly, you asked a question that is relevant and valued by the people in the room as these are school initiatives. Thirdly, you shared that you have a skill set that will add value to this initiative. Lastly, you demonstrated a willingness to make a difference outside the walls of the classroom, possibly in a leadership capacity. WOW! With one thoughtful question, you may have just drastically improved your chances of landing the job! Administrators are always seeking candidates who bring value to the table, both in and out of the classroom. It is up to YOU to communicate the value you bring.

Other questions you may consider asking...

What professional development opportunities are available to your teachers?

This is a great question to ask because it demonstrates your commitment to professional growth and development, which is a critical component of becoming a highly proficient educator.

What are the most important qualities you are seeking in a candidate?

I love this question because it allows you to gain insight on what the school values and what qualities they deem most important. Is it the ability to connect with students and develop a positive rapport? Is it hiring someone who will immerse themselves in the school community and add value both in and out of the classroom? Is it someone who is proficient in using cutting edge technology in the classroom? Regardless of the response, you will gain valuable insight into the mindset of the interviewer(s). This information may prove valuable in a subsequent interview, discussed later in this book.

When reviewing the school's website, I noticed you have two goals… Social Emotional Learning and Using Technology to Enhance Learning. Are there any other initiatives that you are focused on?

Depending on the response, maybe there is an initiative where you have some expertise and can add value. The reason I like this question is that you will learn something about the school that cannot be found on their website. In my experience, the response to this question may be even more powerful than asking about a school goal. Typically, the response provided will be a personal goal for the interviewer and this may have even more importance to that person. Frequently, *school goals* will either come from a committee or be pushed down from the Superintendent or Director of Curriculum. When a principal, for example, is asked an impromptu question about an area of focus they will likely say something that is important to them on a personal level.

Do I have to ask all three questions that I planned in advance? The short answer is, *"No."*

As the interview is approaching the end, you need to read the room and try to get a feel for the interviewer(s). Are they trying to rush you out the door because they have a tight schedule of interviews lined up? Or, are you having an engaging conversation where you feel they are on the edge of their seats?

Read the body language in the room. I cannot stress this enough. If the interviewer appears anxious to wrap things up and is offering brief responses, it is time to stop asking questions. If you are observing overtly positive body language (direct eye contact, sitting upright, and appear eager to hear more) then ask another question. Evaluate your audience after each question to determine if you want to proceed with another question. I know this may sound a bit challenging but once you do it a few times it will not be very difficult. If this is something that is out of your comfort zone, practice at home with a family member or a friend.

Even if the school officials are sitting on the edge of their seats, do not ask more than three questions. There is a specific purpose for the questions you choose to ask. You are hoping to accomplish the following objectives:

1. Demonstrate that you researched their school
2. Gain insight into what they are looking for in a candidate (this information may be useful in your Thank You Letter or a subsequent interview)
3. Acquire information about what they value as a school (this information may be useful in your Thank You Letter or a subsequent interview)

4. Demonstrate your enthusiasm to get involved and immerse yourself in the school community (may include committees, clubs, coaching, etc.)
5. Convey your desire for professional growth

Chapter 4
Thank You Letter

After every interview, send a thank you letter to the interviewer. I am always amazed when I do not receive a thank you letter after an interview. This is a common practice in other professions and definitely applies to education as well. On a basic level, sending the letter/email demonstrates professionalism. I don't want you to settle for basic, however, so I will share some details on how to make your letter leave a lasting impression! The contents of this letter just may be the key to separating you from the competition.

I suggest sending an email on the same day as the interview (in the evening). Same day is prompt and professional, but immediately after the interview is too soon as it doesn't allow time for reflection. Before you begin to write your letter, carefully review your notes from the interview.

Does anything jump out at you?

Maybe you learned something about the school that connected with you. For example, if the school is focusing on Project Based Learning, do some quick research on this strategy to enhance your current knowledge before making mention of it in your thank you letter.

Carefully review the questions you asked at the end of the interview. If you gained insight into what the school is looking for in a candidate, take this opportunity to share how your skill set is in line with their search. If they mentioned a focus on an initiative, talk about how *you* can add value to this initiative! For example, if they talked about reducing out of school suspensions, maybe your previous school was highly effective in this area and you have an idea to share. Maybe you have relevant experience that can contribute to an area of focus… whatever the case, your letter should include some specific detail(s) from the interview and clearly state how you can add value to the school.

Let's look at a possible scenario…

If it was an interview to become an Assistant Principal, and you learned the school has received multiple parent complaints about students being up very late at night due to an abundance of homework. The school is now considering a new homework policy.

What action should you take?

Immediately after the interview, go home and do research! There is unlimited information out there, you just need to access it.

Your thank you letter might include the following blurb...

"I was intrigued by our discussion about students not getting enough sleep and how many of your students are staying up very late doing homework. I found two very interesting articles on teenagers not getting enough sleep and what factors are contributing to this issue. I look forward to discussing this topic in more detail. I have attached the links below."

The key to writing an excellent thank you letter comes down to being <u>relevant</u> and <u>specific</u>. Speaking in generalities is okay for an opening or closing sentence, but you want to quickly get into specific, relevant information from the interview. *Specific* refers to a specific topic or question that was discussed in the interview. *Relevant* means something the person reading the letter actually cares about. Perhaps something he/she stated as an area of focus that is a personal goal. If you are speaking directly about one of the school's initiatives or offering an idea for improvement, he/she will care!

The most effective thank you letters are well thought out, clear and concise. There is no magic formula for how long they should be but at least six sentences and no more than one page. This is a precious opportunity to impress your future employer, so use it wisely.

One last thought about the thank you letter, and this may be the most important piece of the letter. If there was a question that you struggled to answer, **now is your chance to demonstrate your commitment to continuous learning and growth**. Turn a negative into a positive. Hopefully you impressed the interviewer, but maybe that one question that stumped you is still in their head. Look up the question, and craft an intelligent response within your letter.

It might sound something like this…

"I was thinking about the question you asked about tiering a DBQ (Data Based Question), and after reflecting, I would like to elaborate on my response. The first thing I would do is assess the students' ability to comprehend complex text from a primary document…"

This is another excellent opportunity to set yourself apart from the competition. I can tell you firsthand, most people DO NOT do this. They are either too lazy or afraid it will *look bad* if they attempt to expand on one of their responses or attempt to "fix" an incomplete or inaccurate response. Most people hope the interviewer will simply forget about the question they missed or it won't be a big deal. To me, that is ridiculous! Make the extra effort, demonstrate that you really care about this opportunity. If you didn't know something at least you took the initiative to find the answer. This approach is applicable to any profession or industry. None of us are experts in every aspect of our craft; therefore, you must embrace continual growth and always be open to learning new things. Most importantly, this approach speaks to your work ethic, desire to learn and willingness to go the extra mile. Every employer is looking for these qualities in the people they hire! You are not expected to know everything; but if the school values an instructional approach or special program you need to make it a PRIORITY to learn about that program or initiative.

Chapter 5
Second Interview

You got the call for a second interview... now what? First off, congratulations! You impressed your potential employer enough in the first interview that they want to learn more about you. Depending on the position for which you have applied and the philosophy of the school district, you are likely one of three to five candidates being called in for a second interview. If it's a highly coveted position such as a school counselor, there may be more candidates still under consideration. In most cases, however, the second interview narrows the field down to three to five people. As previously stated, these jobs are not easy to land.

Let's reflect on your journey for a minute...

First, you began networking and looking for job openings on the internet. You applied to several schools without even a response from most. Maybe you were fortunate to land a few interviews, but now you are on the precipice of landing a job! This is not the time to take any shortcuts, and certainly not the time to take anything for granted. At this point, you might be the top candidate OR you may have another person ahead of you. Regardless, this is your opportunity to demonstrate that YOU are the best choice for the position.

> In most cases, the second interview will be scheduled 24-48 hours before the actual interview. When you get the call, be sure to confirm the date, time and the location of the interview. In addition, be sure to ask the following questions:
>
> - Who will I be interviewing with?
> - Is there anything I need to bring or present at the interview?

The next 24-48 hours before the interview is critical for two reasons. First, this is your last opportunity to make sure you are fully prepared for BIG DAY #2. The second reason is even more powerful. Never underestimate the power of psychological forces during the interview process. You want the interviewer to be impressed and not have any doubts about you as a candidate. Make sure you are 100% prepared for this interview. Go back to your notes from the first interview and review them carefully.

Was there anything at all that you felt unsure about? If so, look it up and start studying. Become an expert!

You may be thinking that the amount of preparation is a bit excessive, and you might be asking yourself,

"Is all of this really necessary?"

The answer is a resounding *YES*! Remember the correlation between preparation and allowing your true personality to shine in the interview. Do not become a victim of nerves. You have done your homework, you have connected with the interviewers, shared your passion and have established a means to add value to a current initiative. You have come so far in the process, this is your time to close the deal and land the job!

Second Interview Checklist:

- Review portfolio to make sure it is up to date and relevant
- Finalize research on school district
- Review your list of accomplishments (from first interview)
- Review notes from first interview and study any areas that you are uncertain about

I would like to expand upon the last item from the list above...reviewing notes from the first interview. Read these notes carefully. This will give you an understanding of what's important to the administrators and what qualities they are looking for in a candidate. It is highly probable that these topics will be included in the second interview as well. Pay particular attention to the responses they gave to *your* questions. These responses are invaluable.

For example, maybe they are looking for an assistant principal to enforce some new rules and improve the culture in the building. Knowing this information is valuable because you now know to highlight your expertise in this area. Think of specific examples where you made positive contributions to the culture in your school. Also consider how you can get buy-in from the students. Honestly, if this were a real scenario, that would likely be one of the interview questions. Imagine that, reviewing your notes (doing your preparation) may actually lead to you discovering one of the questions that you will be asked!

This exercise of probing into your notes is equally important regardless of the position for which you are preparing for - teacher, counselor or administrator. For a teacher position, the interviewer(s) may have disclosed that Project Based Learning (PBL) is one of their initiatives. Guess what you will be doing before your second interview? Correct! You will be researching/studying PBL until you are confident in your knowledge.

Chapter 6
Demonstration (Demo) Lesson

Your second interview went very well (at least you think it did), you sent a well-crafted thank you letter and two days later you received a call from the school's secretary to schedule a "Demo" Lesson. This is great news! This is most likely the final hurdle to being offered the job.

There will not be a demo lesson for every teaching position and sometimes the time of year (i.e. summer) doesn't make it possible for schools to hold demo lessons. However, in most cases, teachers will be asked to come in and teach a mini lesson as one of the final steps in the hiring process.

When filling a teacher vacancy, I will normally narrow it down to two candidates before having each candidate come in to teach a demo lesson. Some schools include three candidates in the process but regardless this invitation to teach a lesson means you are being seriously considered for the position. The lesson is usually scheduled to be 25-30 minutes in length. This is an opportunity for the administration to observe your teaching style and see you interact with students. When entering a demo lesson, administrators are hoping to get some answers to the following questions…

- Does the candidate have a strong presence in the classroom?
- Is he/she pleasant and respectful to students?
- Is he/she able to connect with students?
- Does he/she have a clear and coherent plan for the lesson?
- If something unexpected happens, how does he/she respond?

Sometimes there are people who are impressive in an interview but fall short in a demo lesson. In my opinion, there is no substitute for a demo lesson. It is a great way to observe creativity, interaction with students, and the candidate's ability to adapt on the fly. After a candidate performs a demo lesson, I will meet with them afterwards. I am always curious to hear a candidate's *reflection* of the lesson. This meeting is usually brief but EXTREMELY IMPORTANT. It is important for a few reasons...

First, this meeting will usually include the supervisor, principal and someone from the central office (maybe even the superintendent). This is likely the first time the candidate has been in a room with all of the key decision makers. When you get here, make sure to bring your A Game!

Second, you can't talk your way around a question. You just spent the last thirty minutes *on stage* in the classroom. Every administrator had the opportunity to see if you practice what you preach. It's one thing to talk the talk but another to walk the walk! Be prepared to discuss what just happened in the classroom as well as a question such as,

"After having met the students and finished the lesson, if you had the chance to do it over again, what would you do differently?"

Third, the administrators will be eager to hear your response to, "So how do you think it went?"

When responding, start with what went well in the lesson before offering what you would change if you had the chance. You should always have something that you offer to change for next time. You want to show that you are reflective and honest. The administrators in the room realize that demo lessons are very hard and they do not expect them to be perfect. The people in the room will respect and appreciate your honesty, especially if you are able to offer some good insight into the lesson.

Demo lessons are hard because you are walking in blind. You do not know the kids, you do not know the classroom setup, and you are expected to go in there and teach a lesson. This is not easy, but there are some things you can do to prepare for a successful demo lesson. After being invited in for a demo lesson, do the following:

1. Contact the department supervisor (or appropriate contact) to get information about the students in the

class. For example... What level are the students in this class (honors, college prep, etc.)? Also ask what prior knowledge the students have with the topic of the demo lesson.

2. Ask about the technology available to you. Incorporating technology in your lesson may enhance your lesson, but it is a risky proposition. This is a personal decision. Make sure you have an alternate plan if the technology doesn't work during the demo lesson.

3. Start planning your lesson. Take a "less is more" approach to your demo lesson. Keep it simple and develop a well thought out plan to engage students for the desired amount of time. There should be an emphasis on being clear and concise during your lesson. Get the students actively involved in the lesson ASAP. Whether you have them talking in groups or moving around the room, you want to get them involved/engaged as soon as possible.

4. Use name cards or some other technique to call students by their first name. This may seem trivial, but you will be able to connect with students by personalizing your interaction with them.

Think about the purpose of this demo lesson from the perspective of the interviewer. The administration at that school has invested a lot of time and energy into their search for a new teacher. They have screened resumes, conducted interviews, had several internal meetings, and they are now hosting two or three demo lessons.

What are they hoping to learn about their finalists during this process? I have broken this question down into four distinct categories:

- Organization/Planning
- Connecting with students
- Command of the classroom
- Ability to adapt (if necessary)

Organization/Planning

All administrators are seeking teachers who are organized and have a strong grasp of planning a lesson. The very first thing that you want to do when you receive the call about a demo lesson is to get as much information as possible. You want to know as much information about the students as possible, including their prior knowledge of the subject matter. You also need to find out what technology will be accessible to you during the lesson. As stated earlier, using technology in a demo lesson can be a risky proposition. However, if you decide that the benefits outweigh the risks, then make sure you have a plan in case the technology does not work.

Even though the demo lesson is usually more of a "mini" lesson, there should still be a logical progression of learning activities and a well-defined structure, similar to that of a traditional lesson. The objective should be clearly stated, there should be a hook to pique the curiosity of the students, there should be high levels of student engagement (whether collaborating in groups or moving around the room), and some type of closure activity. Remember to bring extra hard copies of the lesson to distribute to all observers.

Connecting with Students

Obviously, this will be challenging because you do not know the students or their interests and you are meeting them for the first time. However, there are little things that you can do to make a connection with the students. Make sure to greet the students as they enter the classroom, be polite at all times, and use words such as "please" and "thank you" throughout the lesson. When calling on students, call them by their first names. In addition, consider asking a question that helps you get to know them. Make sure the question has some connection to the content of the lesson. For example, if the demo lesson pertains to heart rate, ask *how many students play a sport or how many exercise regularly.* I am going to warn you, however, to tread lightly. Do NOT go off on a five-minute tangent to get to know what the students are doing in their free time. The demo lesson will go fast! It is important to always keep in mind that you have a short window of time and you need to stay on task. Another approach for connecting with students is personalizing the closure of the lesson. Here are a few examples:

1. Write down one thing you enjoyed during today's lesson
2. Write down one thing you would change about today's lesson
3. Write down one thing you learned in today's lesson

These simple, yet effective closure tasks are intended to get the *students'* perspective. Notice that the word *you* is included in each example to personalize the statement. Like most people, students want to be heard. They want to have a voice and be able to share their opinions. This is an excellent opportunity to get the kids on your side! You may be asking yourself right now, "Why is this important?" Here is a little secret that I will share with you… After every demo lesson, I stay behind (after the candidate leaves) and ask the students to tell me their impression of the candidate. That's right, the STUDENTS may have a strong say in your future employment!

I ask them questions such as:

1. Did you like Mr. or Mrs. Smith? Why or why not?
2. Do you think he/she would be a good fit in our school? Why or why not?

3. What specifically about their lesson did you like/not like?

Lastly, make sure to thank the students and compliment them before leaving the classroom. People like to be praised and students are no different.

Command of the Classroom

Be confident and poised, yet not arrogant or condescending. Speak slowly and clearly; and make sure the students completely understand the objectives of the lesson and what you are asking them to do.

Some of you may be asking, *"How do I remain calm in such a stressful situation?"*

I agree that demo lessons can be very challenging. However, preparation is the key. You need to know this lesson inside out; practice at home and anticipate possible challenges or obstacles. For example, suppose you ask a question and nobody raises their hand. Have a plan for this situation. Get the students involved (actively engaged) early in the lesson. This is never a bad idea and it will also allow you to take a breath to calm yourself. You will be able to relax, walk around the room, and begin to converse with the students.

Ability to Adapt

You will make every effort to ask questions in advance to learn as much as you can about the students. However, you just don't know what to expect until you are in that demo lesson. You will be prepared and have a well-structured lesson; however, there is always a chance that something goes sideways. For example, maybe you were told you would have internet access and your opening activity is showing a short video clip. You better have a solution if the technology doesn't work. If you prepared properly, you will have a plan B. Remain poised and execute your alternate plan. The administrators in the room will undoubtedly be impressed with your planning and your ability to adjust on the fly in the face of adversity.

Another hypothetical scenario that I have seen play out...

After a few minutes, you realize that the lesson you planned is too challenging for this group of students and you notice they are struggling in their groups. Don't panic because you prepared for this possibility. You will break out the guided hints and share them with the groups of students who are struggling. In addition, break down the higher-level questions into smaller chunks (you did this in advance) to help them better understand what is being asked. Taking these additional steps will not only impress the observers in the room but will also demonstrate that you have mastered an important skill in teaching, the ability to adapt.

Key Areas	What to do	What NOT to do
Organization/ Planning	Ask questions to gain as much information as possible; Create a student-centered lesson that maintains a natural progression from beginning to end (it should be clear and concise)	Try to take a 40-minute lesson and squeeze it into a 25-minute time slot; spend more than 5 minutes talking to the students without getting them involved
Ability to connect with students	Call students by their first names; greet students when they enter the room; praise students for correct answers; ask for their opinions and be respectful at all times; use words such as "please" and "thank you"	Address students with words such as "hey you" "buddy" "guys" "pal" etc.; talk down to students; portray yourself as the dictator in the room; act disrespectful in any way including cutting off a student when speaking or using negative phrases such as "no" or "you are wrong"
Command of the classroom/ Presence in the room	Project confidence with a relaxed demeanor; clearly articulate what you want students to do and why; encourage students to work with one another and ask for help if they need it	Coming across as arrogant or condescending; speaking very fast because you are nervous, not being clear with directions and leaving the students wondering "Why are we doing this?"
Ability to adapt (if necessary)	Carefully observe what the students are doing and how well they are grasping the content; have a plan to redirect the lesson if students are struggling to grasp the content; plan for the unexpected including no internet access	Not having a plan if the students are struggling; allowing the students to continue if they are on the wrong track

Chapter 7
Negotiating Salary

When you meet after the demo lesson, it is possible to receive a job offer. In many cases, however, the offer will come later. The superintendent will call or meet with the chosen candidate to make an official offer for employment. The standard rule of thumb is that new teachers (without experience) will be placed on step one of the salary guide. However, every situation is different... think of supply and demand. If the vacant position is an *elementary school teacher*, there is no leverage to negotiate because if you do not accept step one there are likely dozens of qualified candidates who would jump at the opportunity. Elementary positions are extremely competitive so if you land this job, CONGRATULATIONS! Be proud of your accomplishment and take what they offer.

Let's analyze a completely different scenario. You are offered a position to be a High School Physics Teacher, that includes teaching Advanced Placement Physics. Typically, there are very few qualified candidates for this type of specialized position. In this case, even with little or no experience, you will likely have the upper hand in negotiations if you are the chosen candidate. I cannot give you an exact value of what this means but I will say that it is relatively common for this type of position to demand starting on step seven or eight of a salary guide! Again, there are many factors to be considered, including the school's budget, how much they value you, other options available to the school, time of year, etc. Salary guides vary from one school to another and for this position I have seen offers vary as much as $10,000 from one school compared to another! Yet another reason to do your homework.

Think back to where my journey in education began in Bergenfield...

I spent over four hours interviewing for a position as a middle school math teacher. I had no classroom experience but did have work experience that would surely help me in the classroom. They offered step one but I respectfully asked them to consider giving me credit for some of my life and business experiences. I had been out of college for ten years and was hoping to get two or three years of credit for my skill set (i.e. communication skills learned in sales and management positions) and experience working with kids as a coach. We ended up agreeing on *step three* of the guide. I was thrilled! Keep in mind, this was late August and both sides (superintendent and me) were both highly motivated to get a deal done.

There is no magical formula for a starting salary. The superintendent has the authority to start an employee on any step of the guide. However, once you begin working, you are locked into that spot on the guide. I would not suggest being greedy but understand the factors that could influence your starting salary... supply and demand, time of year, subject matter taught and relevant prior experiences.

If you are an aspiring administrator, the starting salary may be more complex. Some districts do not have a guide for administrators so the superintendent has even more discretion. They will definitely have a range in mind, but **how bad they want you** will certainly be an important factor in the job offer and negotiations. Similar to teachers, there are a number of factors that will determine the starting salary and your ability to negotiate more money. The main difference, however, is the leadership responsibilities that come with being an administrator. The other options available to the district and the VALUE they perceive in hiring you will be significant factors in the negotiation.

Chapter 8
Handling Rejection

The Reality Check

It is important to keep perspective on the interview process. For some positions, there may be as many as one hundred applicants. This means, by the numbers, you have about a 1% chance of being the successful candidate. If you are reading this book, and follow all of the suggestions within, your chances will be much better than 1%. However, even if you are well-prepared and ace the interview, there is still a chance that you won't get the job. Sometimes things will be out of your control. The reality is you don't know why you weren't chosen. Maybe they wanted someone with more experience or they chose an internal candidate. In either case, the outcome was out of your control. *Or,* maybe there was something you could have done differently to help your cause. There is only one way to find out - ASK!

As I worked my way up the ladder from Dean of Students to HS Vice Principal to HS Principal, I would always seek out this important feedback. Before landing a position as a vice principal at Hawthorne High School, I finished second at two other schools. Even though this was thirteen years ago, I remember exactly what I was told.

One school told me they chose another candidate because he had more experience than me. I remember feeling so frustrated and defeated. I had been through three grueling rounds of interviews and really felt as though I had connected with the decision makers. I felt frustrated because they knew (from the beginning) that I didn't have any prior high school experience. I felt like if that was going to be a deal breaker, why drag me through three rounds of interviews? This was a situation that was out of my control.

The other school I finished as a runner-up was a high-achieving high school. This time, I was told they wanted someone who was stronger in the area of curriculum. This was a little easier to swallow because at the time, I had very limited teaching experience and had never been through a formal teaching program. I was given specific feedback that I had the power to do something about. Do you know how many curriculum books are out there? Not to mention, there is a ton of curriculum-related information on the New Jersey Department of Education website. The information is there, it is simply a matter of making the time to learn! And that is exactly what I did. After doing so, I was finally comfortable when faced with an interview question about curriculum. In fact, I actually looked forward to it! Knowledge can be so empowering.

You receive a rejection letter or a phone call telling you that they have decided to move forward with another candidate. Even though this is disappointing, it is also an opportunity for growth. I would suggest sending an email to the person who interviewed you as soon as possible requesting a phone conversation (or if that person calls you, ask them for feedback on that call). If there were multiple people in the interview, reach out to the person who you felt most comfortable. Hopefully, there was more than one person you were able to connect with and establish a good rapport. Your email should read something like this:

> "Dear Mrs. J,
>
> I received a letter from Dr. M today that you had decided to move forward with another candidate. I am disappointed but certainly understand that there were other worthy candidates and these decisions are difficult. I really enjoyed my last interview and have a tremendous amount of respect for how you run your school. I am always eager to learn and grow and would greatly appreciate some constructive feedback. Would it be possible to schedule 10 minutes to have a phone conversation one day this week? Thank you for your consideration."

Hopefully you will get the opportunity to learn why you were not the successful candidate. If given the opportunity, listen carefully and take notes on what is being said to you. This information may become extremely useful in the future. We all have a perception of ourselves. We can all list things we perceive as strengths and areas of weakness. However, the perception of others does not always match our own, especially in a potentially stressful environment in an interview with a stranger. You may believe that your passion for teaching and building rapport with students are absolute strengths. However, maybe that did not come across in the interview. Maybe the interviewer got a different impression from you.

Interviews are not only tough on the interviewee, they are also tough on the interviewer. Think about it, they may be conducting as many as 10-15 interviews over three days and based on *only forty-five minutes* they are trying to determine the most deserving people for a second-round interview. I can speak from experience, THIS IS NOT EASY! Many times, administrators are splitting hairs when comparing candidates. Yet another reason to make sure you are fully prepared to put your best foot forward in the interview. You never know what minor detail may be the difference between moving forward in the process or being eliminated from contention.

Never Burn a Bridge

Whether you received the disappointing news that you weren't the successful candidate or you were let go from your current school, the most important piece of advice I can give you is to NEVER BURN A BRIDGE! Like most industries, education is a very small world and administrators talk to one another. We talk at conferences, monthly roundtable meetings, professional development workshops, etc. Since we all have the same challenges, there is quite a bit of collaboration between administrators from different school districts. I am not suggesting that administrators speak negatively about staff that are let go or do not get offered a job. However, when asked about a candidate, if they offer very little, it becomes apparent that the candidate didn't leave a positive impression with the other school district. The last thing you want to do is act disrespectful or unprofessional at any time. You never know when severing a relationship may come back to haunt you.

There is nothing more important than your character, your integrity as a person. Everything from being transparent on that initial application to how you handle disappointing news speaks to your character. Whenever I have the unenviable task of delivering bad news, such as terminating a staff member, I always encourage the employee to stay positive, and do right by the students. Over the years, most people have taken my advice to heart and landed on their feet; unfortunately some did not. I would be willing to bet that those who didn't wish they could have that choice again. It is a matter of taking the emotion out of the situation and checking your ego at the door. Look at the facts of the situation, remain positive and learn from the feedback. It really is as simple as that.

When you leave a school, your next employer will inevitably want to speak to your former supervisor and/or principal. I am not suggesting the previous employer would "bad mouth" you as that would be unprofessional. However, if you leave on bad terms that definitely cannot help you. Administrators are human beings who are influenced by emotions like every other person. Use your remaining weeks at that school to demonstrate your professionalism and character. This may help you in the future. Even though you may be upset with your supervisor or principal, is there any benefit to burning that bridge and leaving on bad terms? Absolutely NOT.

Chapter 9
Conclusion

Not every employer is looking for the same thing for every position they fill. However, there are some qualities that administrators look for, regardless of the position. I say this not only from my own experience, but from speaking with countless other administrators throughout my career in education. The ability to connect with kids, a thirst for knowledge/desire to learn and grow, and the ability to be flexible are essential skills that are highly valued by administrators. Being flexible includes adjusting in the classroom and being open to *feedback*. I challenge you to not only be open to feedback but seek it out! Administrators appreciate when a new teacher invites them into a lesson to observe an "outside the box" approach. Don't be afraid to take a chance. If you have a skill or approach that has been successful in the classroom, share it with your colleagues. Schools need more leaders and leadership does not only come from administrators. I have had the pleasure to work with some amazing teachers who were great leaders within their departments and even schoolwide.

In this book, I walked you through the entire process (from A to Z) of how to land a job in education. My goal was to share my personal experiences and the knowledge I have acquired to help you succeed. My beliefs are based on living through both perspectives (as the interviewee and interviewer) over the past seventeen years as well as countless interactions with other principals.

If you take only one thing away from this book I hope that you understand and value the importance of **preparation**. Preparation is important in every aspect of life whether we are talking about your career, training for a performance, an athletic competition, public speaking, etc. If you expect to just show up at the interview and wing it you are probably going to face disappointment. The interview process has evolved into a complex process over the last twenty-five years with interview committees, multiple rounds of interviews, demo lessons, social media searches and reference checks. However, regardless of what gets thrown your way, you will be prepared if you follow the recommendations outlined in this book.

The competition is fierce and you need to take advantage of every opportunity. Everything from preparing for the interview, what to say/ask during the interview, and the appropriate follow up will set you apart from the crowd. There are several tools covered in this book, it is now time to put them to use.

Knowledge of your craft is important, studying possible interview questions is important, being familiar with your biggest accomplishments is important, and being nice to the secretaries is also important. *A LOT* of things are important; however, the MOST IMPORTANT thing is for you to relax and allow your true self and passion to shine through during this process! A confident (not arrogant) and relaxed candidate will perform the best in the interview. Confidence and the ability to relax is directly correlated to your level of PREPARATION. Once you are able to relax, the interview will flow freely and be more conversational. You have done the work, you know your stuff… share your passion and let them get to know the real you.

Follow the steps in this book and make the most of your opportunity!

Made in the USA
Monee, IL
11 March 2022